Connecting with Christ

Connecting with Christ

Kate Lee

DESERET BOOK

© 2023 Kate Lee
Artwork by Kate Lee

All rights reserved. No part of this book may be reproduced in any form or by any means without permission in writing from the publisher, Deseret Book Company, at permissions@deseretbook.com. This work is not an official publication of The Church of Jesus Christ of Latter-day Saints. The views expressed herein are the responsibility of the author and do not necessarily represent the position of the Church or of Deseret Book Company.

DESERET BOOK is a registered trademark of Deseret Book Company.

Visit us at deseretbook.com

Library of Congress Cataloging-in-Publication Data
(CIP data on file)
ISBN 978-1-63993-135-4

Printed in China
RR Donnelley, Dongguan, China

10 9 8 7 6 5 4 3 2 1

For Mike, Jackson, and Cooper,

Thank you for your incredible support
and for believing in me
especially when I forgot to.
Having the three of you
by my side made this all possible.
I love you more than you know.

Also, a huge thank you
to my friends Joanna, Rachael, Travis,
Courtney, Steve, Emily, Dave, Julie, Casey,
Zerelda, Lee, Brad, Derek, Dallan,
Celia, and President Wasden
for cheering me on
through this entire process.
Love you all so much.

Contents

Foreword by Emily Belle Freeman ix

Introduction 1

Chapter One: Connected with Christ 5

Chapter Two: I Am Enough 15

Chapter Three: Flaxen Cords 23

Chapter Four: Through His Light 29

Chapter Five: Peace in Christ 37

Chapter Six: Father Bless Them 45

Chapter Seven: Receiving Strength from Above 53

Chapter Eight: Hold Up Your Light 61

Chapter Nine: The Atonement 67

Chapter Ten: Come unto Me 75

Notes 85

Foreword

I met Kate several years ago. We spent the afternoon together. What I remember about that first encounter was her genuine heart and the way she offered her friendship with both gentleness and strength. When I opened the pages of this book, it was like spending an afternoon with Kate again to talk about my most favorite topic—Jesus.

Kate comes from a place of deep vulnerability as she shares her journey of coming to know Christ. She weaves her feelings of doubt, lack, and greatest need through a framework of peace, light, and healing, creating a beautiful masterpiece of love. As I read her own personal touchpoints with the Savior, I was able to pause and ponder my own. Her story begins with a struggle we are all familiar with—*am I enough?*—and ends with the power of grace that comes through the Atonement of Jesus Christ. Each chapter is bookended with a piece of artwork and questions to ponder, and the journaling thoughts that came as I read will make this book a treasure for years to come.

Perhaps you have a great desire to know Jesus Christ better. Maybe you wonder where to start, or how to begin. These words walked me through that process in the gentle yet strengthening way that I have come to love about Kate.

Several years ago, one of my dearest friends passed away. It was a friend who had helped me to know Jesus Christ better. I reached out to Kate and asked if she would paint a piece that would capture my friend's reunion with Christ. She asked a lot of questions and then began the process of creating the piece I had requested. A few days later, she and her husband drove to the city where I live. We walked over to my friend's home and sat with her husband as she unveiled the painting. It was such a tender experience. One I will never forget. And the fact that she drove hours to where I was to drop off the gift made it even sweeter.

I hope that is what this book will be for you. An afternoon spent with Kate. A treasured moment where you can sit with her beautiful artwork and listen to her gentle yet strong testimony of Jesus Christ.

These words will lead you closer to Him.

That is the greatest gift of all.

—Emily Belle Freeman
December 2022

Introduction

I've always known Christ is real, but you might be surprised to learn that I didn't always believe that His life and His Atonement were meant for me. For many years I believed that the person I am was unworthy. Unworthy of love, unworthy of someone's time, unworthy of friendship, unworthy of compassion, understanding, forgiveness, hope, peace, and especially unworthy of God and His Son Jesus Christ.

I remember sitting in Primary, Young Women, seminary, the Missionary Training Center, and Relief Society and being taught about Christ—about His love for each of us and how He died for each of us. Although I loved learning about the Savior, I struggled to believe that His love and Atonement included me. I would often leave those lessons feeling a little hopeless inside. I wanted so much to feel like the messages applied to me and my life. I didn't realize it at the time, but I was walking through this life without allowing the light and love of Jesus Christ to be a part of my day-to-day experiences.

My understanding of who I am as a daughter of God and the role Christ can play in my life changed in October 2014, when I made an appointment with my stake president to renew my temple recommend. I had no idea what was coming or the plan that Heavenly Father had in store for me. I walked into my stake president's office on a Sunday morning, we went through the questions, and he signed my recommend. As I got up to leave, the stake president stopped me and asked, "Kate, is there anything else you want to talk about?"

I quickly told him, "No, I'm okay, but thank you so much."

I started to walk out again, only to have him say, "Kate, is there anything else you need to talk about?"

The word *need* stopped me in my tracks. I didn't want to talk about anything, but I needed to talk about everything. I couldn't stop the tears from pouring down my cheeks as I expressed every negative thought or feeling I had about myself. I told him my past experiences that were weighing me down, how unworthy I felt, and how I was certain that the Savior didn't love me. We sat in his office and talked. He testified to me of Christ's personal love for me. He told me that Jesus knew me and was waiting for me to reach out to Him so He could heal me. He pointed at a painting of Christ in his office and asked me what I felt when I looked at the Savior. I don't remember what I said, but I do remember that as I looked at this painting, my heart calmed, I felt warmth and light, and the Spirit testified to me that I was loved. It was exciting, and I wanted to hold on to that feeling. I felt like Alma the Younger when he realized what the Savior and His Atonement could do for him (see Mosiah 27). Sweetness and joy began to replace my pain.

Introduction

Talking with my stake president and allowing all of my pain to be heard helped me to open my heart to my Savior and to finally make room for Him and His Atonement in my life. I left that office lighter, feeling new hope. I was looking forward to building a better, deeper, and more personal relationship with Heavenly Father and Jesus Christ. It wasn't an overnight transformation. Learning that I mattered to Them and discovering how to include Christ in my daily life has taken time, trust, personal patience, and faith. I've had to break lifelong habits of telling myself I don't matter and replace them with new, healthier habits. I've had to revisit old pain and learn how to take that pain to the Lord. I've had to learn how to break down the walls I built around myself. I've had to practice looking to Him for direction instead of to the world. It hasn't been easy, but with Christ, it has been possible.

Allowing Jesus's light into my life has helped me know that I am loved, I am known, and I have purpose. I know I am not the only one who has faced the struggle of feeling unworthy of Christ and the peace He offers. My hope is that as you read this book, you can feel closer to Him; that you can come to know the Savior and know for yourself that you are important to Him. The things you face and the loads you carry are known and understood. I hope you can start to see yourself the way He sees you. I hope that you can feel your Father in Heaven and Savior close to you as you read this book, and especially as you walk through your daily life.

You are loved, you are known, and you have purpose.

I invite you to open your heart and enjoy this journey.

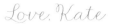

Love, Kate

Chapter One

Connected with Christ

I sat in my studio with a blank piece of watercolor paper in front of me, wanting to paint something that represented the connection we share with our Savior—something that would show how committed Christ is to us personally. As I pondered this great truth, I envisioned Christ with His hand up, reaching out to connect with us. As I painted, I tried to imagine myself standing there with my hand meeting His. The experience led me to do a self-inventory of the things I was trying to do to show my Savior that I loved Him, as well as the things I needed to change. I asked myself, "Am I allowing Christ to be connected with me and myself with Him? Am I keeping Him at arm's length? Am I too scared to develop the kind of connection I hope for? Do I trust Him?"

Connecting with our Savior means being vulnerable. It means learning to trust His personal and perfect love for us. We naturally want to hide the things about ourselves we feel are weaknesses and show only our strengths, but if we share only our strengths with the Lord, we cannot grow, progress, change, and overcome. If we never allow our Heavenly Father and our Savior to connect with us, we will only stand still.

I love what the Lord says in Ether 12:27: "And if men come unto me I will show unto them their weakness. I give unto men weakness that they may be humble; and my grace is sufficient for all men that humble themselves before me; for if they humble themselves before me, and have faith in me, then will I make weak things become strong unto them."

Our Heavenly Father and Savior are calling us to Them. When I read this scripture, I can feel Their deep desire for us to fully turn to Them and allow ourselves to be vulnerable with Them, even when it's difficult. They love us and want us to become who we are meant to become. This scripture is a perfect recipe for us to learn how to open ourselves up and be vulnerable and honest so that we can have that true and pure connection with Them.

One of the greatest examples in my life of someone striving to stay close and connected to Christ was my friend Kjarsta. Every time we spoke, she always brought the conversation back to our Redeemer. No matter what she was facing or how heavy her load was, she knew she could find her strength through the Savior.

I met Kjarsta when I was a new missionary. She was my senior companion. The moment I met her, I could feel her connection with and testimony of Christ. There was something different about her. She read her scriptures differently, said her prayers differently, and talked about the Savior like she knew Him. I would watch in awe as she would share her testimony of Jesus Christ with the people around her. I wanted to know and love Him the way she did.

One day I asked her how she knew the Savior so well and how she stayed so close to Him. She said, "It's a daily effort, but I know that He loves me perfectly." I didn't understand her words then. I wish I had. I went on watching her in amazement, wishing I could have a connection with the Lord the way she did, all the while telling myself that I wasn't worthy of a connection like hers. Have you told yourself this before? Are you telling yourself this now?

When Kjarsta returned home from her mission, she continued to share her testimony of Christ with those around her through the example of her unwavering faith. She faced many challenges that tested her and that could have easily threatened her connection with the Savior if she had allowed them to. However, she knew that with and through Jesus Christ, she could make it through the challenges she faced.

With permission from her family, I want to share the rest of her story. One of Kjarsta's greatest desires was to get married and become a mother. In 2009, she married her sweetheart, Kristian. In 2016, they were living in Washington and had welcomed four beautiful children into their family. In November of that year, while pregnant with their fifth child, Kjarsta experienced intense headaches that would not go away. She was soon diagnosed with brain cancer and was given the option to terminate her pregnancy in order to move forward with cancer treatments. But, with faith in God's plan for her family, she chose not to end the pregnancy. She delivered a healthy baby boy in April of 2017. For a time, the cancer didn't appear to grow or change, and after radiation therapy, all that remained was to wait and see.

Nagging in the back of Kjarsta's mind and heart was a feeling that there was a spirit missing in the family: a little girl. She didn't know why she felt so strongly that she needed to have one more baby, but she could not shake the thought. She also could not shake the thought that her cancer was likely to return in the future. Kjarsta was scared and didn't want to risk losing her life and having her five children grow up without her, but she ultimately decided that she needed to bring another baby into the world, that there was a bigger plan, and that all would be okay.

Kjarsta soon became pregnant, and for the first twenty weeks, everything looked great. However, about two weeks into the second trimester, an MRI scan showed the cancer had ballooned in size and a new surgery was needed. Despite her fear, Kjarsta faced the surgery with the calm assurance that she was doing what she was supposed to do and that in the end, it would all work out. Again her medical team discussed the fact that her cancer treatment would benefit if she terminated the pregnancy, but Kjarsta was firm that this baby was meant to be in the family, and she was willing to sacrifice so this little one could come to earth. She stayed connected to Christ and trusted God's plan.

During this pregnancy, the cancer grew at an alarming rate, and at thirty weeks it was decided that Kjarsta would deliver their beautiful baby girl. There would still be mountains to climb for Kjarsta and her family, but they did it all while holding tightly to the knowledge that with and through the Savior they could have the strength they needed to make it to the other side. Kristian said to me, "We all kept faith that there would be a miracle. Kjarsta was a faithful woman who followed the commandments. If anyone deserved a miracle, it was her. Kjarsta got her miracle. She lived longer than was expected with the prognosis. She brought two wonderful, healthy babies into the world. She changed the lives of everyone she met for the better, and her legacy continues to this day."

My sweet friend Kjarsta passed away on September 24, 2019, nearly three years after she was first diagnosed with brain cancer. In her passing, she leaves a legacy of faith and hope. Her example testifies that staying connected with Christ is a choice.

I look back on the time we served together as missionaries and I see now that I didn't know the Savior the way she did because I hadn't learned to trust in the Savior the way she had. I have learned through time, experience, and the example she continues to set for me that having that connection with Christ and staying connected with Him requires me to give all of my trust to Him, putting my everything—ALL of who I am—into His hands. That isn't always easy, especially if you feel unseen by Christ. But remember, building that connection with the Lord requires vulnerability, trust, and faith. It requires us to lay aside the things of this world and seek something better (see D&C 25:10). If you feel your connection with the Savior is lacking strength, take time to do a self-inventory. What are you doing that is deepening your connection with Him, and what can you let go of that might be keeping you from Him?

Consider these questions as you study this painting. What do you feel and why? What do you hope for?

I love the way the woman is looking up at Christ. There is so much trust in her gaze, as if to say to Him, "I know you are my Savior." I love that their hands are pressed together. I feel like she is giving her ALL to Christ. I hope to give my all to Him.

Jesus Christ loves you. He wants you to know Him. Through Him, we find our courage, strength, hope, peace, rest, understanding, purpose, and direction. You are His. Do all you can to stay connected with Him.

Remember the scripture: "Fear not, little children, for you are mine, and I have overcome the world, and you are of them that my Father hath given me; and none of them that my Father hath given me shall be lost. . . . Wherefore, I am in your midst, and I am the good shepherd, and the stone of Israel. He that buildeth upon this rock shall never fall" (D&C 50:41–42, 44).

Questions

What can I do to strengthen my connection with Christ?

What can I let go of that might be keeping me from Him?

Chapter Two

I Am Enough

In May 2001, I was sitting on an airplane headed for the Preston England Missionary Training Center, excited yet scared to death of what I was about to do. I knew I was supposed to serve a mission—there was no doubt about that. However, my mind was filled with doubts about my abilities, and I questioned whether I'd be an effective missionary. I remember saying to myself, "How on earth can I even do this? I hardly know anything about the gospel. I have never read the Book of Mormon cover to cover. There are better people for this job. Am I enough?"

Part of me wanted to stop the plane, jump off, and run away, but I held on to the one thing I was absolutely certain of: God wanted me to serve a mission. For the next twelve hours, my emotions went back and forth from excitement to absolute fear and silent crying (I feel so sorry for the poor person who sat next to me). When the plane landed in England,

I took a deep breath, got up, and walked forward, trusting God's plan for me.

Those eighteen months were amazing and challenging and rewarding. There were dark days when doubt dictated my actions, and there were bright days when I felt like nothing could take me down. The idea of serving a mission had terrified me. I worried I would ruin the work in England, but God knew better. He knew what serving a mission could and would do for me personally. He understood my fear and He gently took my hand and taught me what I was capable of. Serving a mission was exactly what I needed to move forward in my life. It was my very first step in understanding that who I am and what I have to offer is enough.

The experiences of my mission gave me ground to stand on and a well of hope to draw from. They shined a new light in my life and helped strengthen my understanding of Christ. Although I began my mission full of fear and doubt in my abilities, I learned that it didn't matter how much or how little I knew; it only mattered that I put my trust in God and walked forward in faith. I came home happier, with more confidence and a better understanding of who I was. I have tried hard to hold on to the experiences from my mission and to remember that I am enough and that with my Heavenly Father and Savior's help, I can become more like Them.

A few years ago, I sat with and listened to a sweet young woman as she shared with me how she wished she could be enough. She told me it was hard for her to want to get up each day and face things because she hated feeling that she was letting everyone down. She asked me how she could get to a place where she could be enough. Her question broke my heart. How could this amazing young woman not know that she was a loved and needed daughter of God? I looked at her and told her that she was already enough and that God believed in and loved her.

Together we read Doctrine and Covenants 18:10, which says, "Remember the worth of souls is great in the sight of God." I told her that this scripture was talking about her. I told her that she mattered to her Heavenly Father and to Jesus Christ and that They didn't want her to go through life suffering and doubting her worth, but that They wanted her to remember and know how important she is. I invited her to pray and ask Heavenly Father to teach her so she could know for herself that she was enough. Then, with the help of heaven, she could reach her greatest potential.

After our conversation, week after week I saw the light come into this young woman's eyes as she learned her true worth. She was enough, and she was making a difference in the lives of those around her.

The adversary works hard to convince us that we are worthless. That is his game. He will do everything he can to get us to forget who we are and what we came here to do. He wants to distract us so we miss opportunities to grow. He knows that when we turn to God and our Savior and place our lives in Their hands, everything can change for the better. Satan doesn't want us to be successful or happy here. He wants us to focus on what we are not instead of seeing what God and Christ see. We were sent here on purpose, with purpose.

The parable of the sower is one of my favorite passages in scripture. In Mark 4:14 we read, "The sower soweth the word." This is Christ teaching us truth, giving us light. But then we learn in verse 15, "Satan cometh immediately, and taketh away the word that was sown in their hearts."

Doesn't that just make you crazy? Where Jesus Christ is constantly reaching out and giving us light and reminding us of who we are, Satan is constantly trying to block that light and take it from us.

When I read verse 15 for the first time, I was frustrated knowing that Satan was working so hard to take the Savior's light from the world. I remember thinking, "What can I do to fight against Satan's efforts?" At that moment, I determined to seek Christ's light through the scriptures, prayer, conference talks, and spending time in nature. I wanted to share His light with others through my paintings. Reaching out to friends during difficult times and allowing myself to be vulnerable with them helped me to remember who I am and to push back on Satan's lies. I told myself that no matter how big or small my effort might be, it counted. I knew I would gain personal and spiritual strength with every step forward. Of course, there are still times when I give in to those doubts, question my worth, and fall short in sharing Christ's light, but I know when I turn to my Heavenly Father and Savior, They are right there to pick me back up and remind me that I have a place with Them.

In 2018, our stake was getting ready for a Young Women camp. The theme was "I Am Enough." I was asked to paint a picture for the girls, one that would help remind them of the lessons they would learn throughout the week. I thought about this for a while. I wanted the painting to capture our camp theme perfectly. When an image came to my mind of a young girl looking up toward heaven with her hands open to offer all of who she is to her Heavenly Father, I knew it was the symbol we needed.

As I drew this idea out, I saw not only the girl offering her whole self to Heavenly Father, but I could also see Him reaching back toward her and offering strength, hope, knowledge, peace, love, and comfort. It taught me again that Heavenly Father is aware of and personally invested in us. He wants us to know who we are.

When we turn to our Heavenly Father and offer all of who we are, it is not just a one-way road. Heavenly Father is always there listening to us and watching over us. He is constantly giving us strength so we can know for ourselves that we are enough. Through Him and our Savior, we can reach our fullest potential.

Questions

What experiences have you had that have helped you know that you are enough?

How will you hold on to those experiences?

Chapter Three

Flaxen Cords

In John 16:33, the Lord proclaims, "These things I have spoken unto you, that in me ye might have peace. In the world ye shall have tribulation: but be of good cheer; I have overcome the world." This scripture makes my heart rejoice every time I read it. It's comforting to know that even though we will experience tribulation in this life, we have a Savior who has overcome it all.

In President Thomas S. Monson's conference talk "I Will Not Fail Thee, Nor Forsake Thee" from October 2013, he taught, "Only the Master knows the depths of our trials, our pain, and our suffering. He alone offers us eternal peace in times of adversity. He alone touches our tortured souls."

I was thirty-five years old before I understood what it truly meant to reach out and up to the Savior. I had had experiences with Christ's

Atonement before, and I knew that was where I would find peace and strength, but I had a bad habit of telling myself I wasn't worthy, so I limited myself. Reaching out to Christ felt a little awkward and uncomfortable. Sharing my artwork with those around me also felt awkward and uncomfortable. I have always loved drawing and painting, and they have been part of me for as long as I can remember, but I rarely dared to share my work with those around me due to my fear of rejection. My heart yearned to share what I had created, and it yearned to know Jesus better, but fear had the upper hand until my experience painting *Flaxen Cords*.

In February 2015, my stake president handed me a piece of paper with a scripture reference on it: 2 Nephi 26:22. He said to me, "Kate, I want you to paint me a picture based on this scripture." I immediately told him no and explained that I wasn't good enough to paint something like that. His response was, "Yes you are and yes you can. I'm excited to see what you come up with."

I sat for a moment and thought, "I could say no and walk away from this, or I could step outside of my comfort zone and learn something new."

I wanted change in my life, and I knew this was an opportunity for exactly that, so I took a deep breath, put my fear aside, held out my hand, took that piece of paper, and read the scripture: "And there are also secret combinations, even as in times of old, according to the combinations of the devil, for he is the founder of all these things; yea, the founder of murder, and works of darkness; yea, and he leadeth them by the neck with a flaxen cord, until he bindeth them with his strong cords forever."

I went home that evening and started drawing up ideas. It took me nine months to draw up, paint, and finally finish the painting.

Those nine months were a roller coaster of emotions. They were a mix of turmoil and peace. I fought against the assignment and for the assignment. I was mad at God and thankful that He had placed this opportunity in my path. I cried because it seemed too hard, and I cried because of what I was gaining and how I was growing.

After months of free-falling, one day I felt ground under me, and I started to feel more peace than turmoil. I started to feel more desire to paint. I noticed the doubts were quieter and my confidence was growing. Those flaxen cords that had been wrapped around me for so long had started to lose their grip and fall away, and I started to see myself differently. I started to understand Christ's Atonement more fully.

I noticed I had opened my heart more to the Savior, and that I began to give to Him, little by little, the loads I had been holding on to. Instead of looking down, giving in to my doubts and holding on to my pain, I started to look up and reach out for Christ and His light. I started to let go and trust the Savior more. I recognized that my focus was changing. Christ's hands were stretched out toward me, and for the first time, I understood that He wanted me to reach back. So I did.

This beautiful invitation from my stake president, as scary as it was, put me in a position where I learned to start trusting the Lord and the peace He so earnestly wants to give. I learned to start trusting myself and the talent God has given me. I learned how to open up to the Spirit more and how to better lay aside my insecurities and fears and seek help from above. I learned that God and Christ are in the details of our lives and that they are giving us opportunities to grow and to break those flaxen cords every day.

The invitation to paint flaxen cords gave me courage to reach into the heart of my fear. It taught me that I could do those things that scared me. It showed me that I could paint and share what was in my heart. It helped me develop a greater relationship with my Heavenly Father and the Savior—and with myself. I'm not sure if my stake president planned it that way, but his invitation to paint a picture about flaxen cords helped me overcome my fear of sharing my art and my fear of reaching out to Christ.

Questions

What are the flaxen cords in your life that are holding you back?

What will you do to help break your flaxen cords and remind yourself to reach for Christ?

Chapter Four

Through His Light

The first time I accepted that my Heavenly Father and Savior loved me personally was when I prayed over sticky notes. A friend had asked me to write down on sticky notes what I thought was true about me. I hesitated. I did not want to write anything down. I did not want anyone to see what I thought the truth about me was because I was terrified that they'd agree with what I wrote down. I knew my friend had good intentions in asking me to be open and vulnerable, but I wasn't sure I was ready for that. I was used to holding on to negative feelings about myself, and being asked to step out of that safe zone scared me.

I sat there looking at the sticky notes for what felt like forever, debating whether or not to do this. However, I trusted my friend and knew he was trying to help me, so I picked up the pen in front of me and started to write.

On the first sticky note, I wrote down, "You are dumb." On the next, "You are a disappointment to your family," and then, "No one likes you," "You are ugly," "You are not a good mom," "You are bad at your calling," and "You are in the way." None of them were super uplifting thoughts.

Tears streamed down my face as I wrote on each sticky note. These beliefs had been stuck inside of me my whole life. Writing them out on pieces of paper and seeing them in front of me stung deeply. It was a painful reminder of how much I wanted to be a good person and to have worth but constantly felt like I didn't. That raw moment of allowing myself to step away from my safe zone and finally face these things that were actually lies opened a door of healing for me.

When I finished writing on the sticky notes, my friend smiled at me and then pulled out more sticky notes as he said, "Thank you so much for writing that down. But now, Kate, write the truth."

I looked at him and said, "What are you talking about? That is the truth. That is who everyone sees, including God."

He looked at me and said with a stern but tender voice, "No, it's not. You are so much more than this."

Every time I think back to that moment and those words, I think of President Boyd K. Packer's teaching: "Don't you realize who you are? Haven't you learned yet that you are a son or daughter of Almighty God?"[1] Up to that point in my life, I hadn't realized that, but Heavenly Father did, and He was about to teach me.

My friend challenged me to take the sticky notes home and pray about each one of them and listen to what the Spirit would teach me. I took them home and set them aside for a few days. I was nervous to take them to God.

One morning, while I was helping my boys get ready for school, I had a quiet prompting that it was a good day to pick up those sticky notes and take them to Heavenly Father. I felt a little sick to my stomach at the thought, but I was ready.

After I sent my boys off to school, I walked over to where I had left those sticky notes, picked them up, went over to our couch, and knelt down. I didn't know what I was going to say, but I closed my eyes and began to pray. The only words I got out clearly were "Dear Heavenly Father." The rest of the time was spent crying and pleading with God for relief and understanding.

I don't know how long I knelt there at our couch, but it was a while. During the prayer, my tears went from total heartbreak and sorrow to hope and comfort as I felt a warm blanket of peace gently fall over me. I remember my mind being filled with positive words about the person I am and how Heavenly Father and the Savior see me. I went from feeling unworthy to feeling light, from feeling lost to having peace. I stood up from that prayer a new person. I knew that Heavenly Father and the Savior were aware of me and my needs. I knew They had sat with me as I cried and as I started to understand who I am through the Spirit.

In Ether 2:24, the Lord says, "For behold, ye shall be as a whale in the midst of the sea; for the mountain waves shall dash upon you. Nevertheless, I will bring you up again out of the depths of the sea."

Heavenly Father and Christ are aware of you. When you feel lost, beaten, unworthy, forgotten, or unseen, They are there sitting with you.

Take a minute and look at the painting in this chapter. One of my favorite things about this painting is how Christ's hands are under the girl's hands, giving her support. It reminds me of the promise found in Doctrine and Covenants 84:88: "I will go before your face. I will be on your right hand and on your left, and my Spirit shall be in your hearts, and mine angels round about you, to bear you up."

I love how He is sitting with her, helping her as she starts to understand who she is, and I love the light that is surrounding them. Christ is our Savior, and through His light, broken hearts can be healed, deep pain can be lifted, and love can be felt and understood.

I want to extend the sticky note invitation to you. I invite you to be raw and vulnerable. Ask Heavenly Father for strength as you write down on your sticky notes what you think is true about you. Don't be afraid to write down your heaviest feelings. When you are finished writing, I invite you to take those sticky notes to your Father in Heaven and ask Him to teach you the truth about who you really are. As you pray, listen to what the Spirit will teach you.

When have you felt Christ near?

How can allowing Christ's light into your life change you?

Chapter Five

Peace in Christ

Peace in Christ is one of my favorite paintings. I love how it came to be and how it makes me feel when I look at it.

In February 2018, I got a message from a friend in Oklahoma asking me if I could paint something for a very specific need. She shared her struggle with multiple sclerosis and the strength she found through her husband, who promised to carry her wherever she needed to go. She said that his commitment to her helped heal her heart and strengthen her trust and relationship with her Savior. I cried as I listened to her share her story of heartbreak and peace. While she talked, this beautiful image of her being cradled and carried came into my mind.

As I drew out and painted this picture, the Spirit testified to me more than once that Christ loves my sweet friend and that He also feels that same love for me and for each of us. The Spirit filled my studio that day.

Painting *Peace in Christ* helped to solidify my testimony even more that the Savior lived and died for each of us so we could overcome all things. It helped me better understand the willingness of Christ to lift and carry us through the experiences we face in this life. It taught me that He is there even and especially when we feel unseen.

I love these words from President Dieter F. Uchtdorf: "Though we are incomplete, God loves us completely. Though we are imperfect, He loves us perfectly. Though we may feel lost and without compass, God's love encompasses us completely."[2]

These words make me think of Ted Wilmoth. I met Ted while I was a missionary. My companion and I were out knocking on doors in Bayswater, London, when this small, frail, older man with a walker opened the door. He smiled brightly at us and invited us in. He offered us a drink of orange juice, invited us to sit down, and asked us about ourselves. We told him who we were and what we were doing and asked him about himself. He shared with us some of the experiences of his life, about his family, and how grateful he was just to be alive. We learned that he had recently lost his wife and how lonely he'd been and how glad he was to have someone to talk to again. We instantly loved this man and made plans to come and visit again.

We visited Ted every week. Each time we came he would have a list of questions for us about God, Christ, and the scriptures, and we would do our best to answer them all. Ted already had a belief in God, but he felt forgotten. After his wife passed away, he had spent his days alone, with no family or neighbors stopping by to visit him. During one of our visits, he told us that he was ready to give up and then we knocked on his door. I am so grateful we were led to his door that day.

An amazing thing happened with Ted. My companion and I watched a beautiful transformation take place within him as he learned about the Savior and His Atonement. We watched light come into Ted's eyes. We saw his countenance change and his perspective on life brighten. Ted started to understand that he wasn't alone. He started to understand that his Heavenly Father and Savior loved him. He started to turn to Them and find peace in Them. He was so motivated and passionate about what he was learning, he wanted to share it with everyone. And he did. Ted was baptized in the Hyde Park Chapel in London ten months after we first knocked on his door.

We watched him as he went from being sad, alone, and in need of a walker to getting out of his chair without assistance, going out, and running his errands again. He got himself to church and eventually traveled the world, including making multiple visits to Utah to visit his "American granddaughters" before he passed away a few years ago.

Ted Wilmoth was a beloved son of God who felt alone and forgotten, but because of Jesus Christ's Atonement, he learned he wasn't. He learned to turn to his Father in Heaven and Savior, and through Them he found peace.

Last summer I was reminded yet again that peace can be found when we turn to the Savior. I was standing in a hotel pool crying to my husband Mike because the weight of my depression felt too heavy. We were on vacation—it was supposed to be a carefree time—and even though I was trying to be carefree, I wasn't feeling it on the inside. In my mind, I was failing. Failing at motherhood, failing with friendships, failing at my calling, just straight-up failing.

It was difficult to feel like myself. It was as if I had a thick fog over my head that was keeping me from seeing and feeling any light, and moving forward felt almost impossible.

I stood there in that hotel pool feeling a bit broken and a little lost, and my sweet Mike stood right there with me and listened to every word I said. When I was finished talking, he pulled me into a tight hug and said, "I am right here with you every step of the way, and even though it's difficult now, the fog will lift and lose its strength and you will be able to walk forward."

He was right. That struggle, that thick fog, lifted and lost its strength, and the peace I needed came.

I have thought about that experience with Mike in that hotel pool over and over again as other obstacles have crossed my path. I have imagined the Savior standing there with me and saying, "I am right here with you every step of the way, and even though it's difficult now, the fog will lift and lose its strength and you will be able to walk forward."

Christ understands our struggles perfectly. He knows the hurt, the loneliness, the despair you feel. He will give you peace as you turn to Him. I love what He says in Matthew 11:28–30: "Come unto me, all ye that labour and are heavy laden, and I will give you rest. Take my yoke upon you, and learn of me; for I am meek and lowly in heart: and ye shall find rest unto your souls. For my yoke is easy, and my burden is light."

You are not alone. You are not forgotten. You are heard and seen. Christ is there to help us push past the fog and see His light and receive His peace.

Questions

What does "peace in Christ" mean to you?

What loads are you holding on to that you can give to the Savior?

Chapter Six

Father Bless Them

I love the experience found in the Book of Mormon when Christ visits the people in the Americas. In 3 Nephi 8 we learn about the tempests, earthquakes, fires, whirlwinds, physical upheavals, and how a thick darkness covered the land for three days prior to His appearance.

In chapter 9, in that darkness, Christ speaks to the people. In verse 13, He invites them to come unto Him and be converted, that He may heal them.

In chapter 10, Christ speaks to them again and the darkness is lifted. Their mourning and weeping turn to rejoicing and thanksgiving. Then, in chapter 11, we learn how Heavenly Father spoke unto the people and testified of Christ and learn that they all looked up and saw the Savior descending.

For a moment, everything had seemed lost and hopeless. People's hearts were broken and they were scared. And then Jesus Christ came. He taught them. He gave them hope and comfort. He healed them one by one. He stayed with them and prayed for them. The impact of His presence was so powerful that when He said it was time for Him to go, the people wept, so Christ stayed a little longer because He loved them.

This account always brings me to the experience of young Joseph Smith, who prayed in the Sacred Grove. He shares in Joseph Smith—History 1:15–17:

> After I had retired to the place where I had previously designed to go, . . . I kneeled down and began to offer up the desires of my heart to God . . . , when immediately I was seized upon by some power which entirely overcame me. . . . Thick darkness gathered around me, and it seemed to me for a time as if I were doomed to sudden destruction. But, exerting all my powers to call upon God to deliver me out of the power of this enemy which had seized upon me, and at the very moment when I was ready to sink into despair and abandon myself to destruction . . . , I saw a pillar of light . . . which descended gradually until it fell upon me. . . . I found myself delivered from the enemy which held me bound.

These experiences teach us that no matter how dark or difficult things get, our Heavenly Father and our Savior will never abandon us. They are there ready to bless, teach, love, and bring us out of darkness through Their light.

A dear friend of mine shared her experience with me of heartbreak, loneliness, and feeling God's love. With her permission, I share it with you.

February 7, 2020, was a heartbreaking day for me. It was the first time I felt something I would soon recognize as indescribable loneliness. For the first time, my kids left to spend the weekend with their dad. As they drove away, feelings I didn't know existed overcame my entire body as I realized this was my new normal. From this day on I would share my kids. They would spend days at a time away from me, and I would be left alone.

I struggled with severe loneliness for months. Daytime was difficult, but being alone at night was excruciating. Sometimes I would cry until every cell in my body was used up. Other times I would lie there completely numb. I felt shredded inside. Guilt was a close companion. What had we done? Was divorce right? Should we have tried to stay together? We had been married for nineteen years; for what? For it to just end. I felt anger. Why me? Why couldn't he choose me? I felt abandoned, and I started to wonder if God had also abandoned me. Where was He? Why hadn't He stepped in with a miracle and saved my marriage? Why was He leaving me alone in my darkest moment?

The only time I felt peace was in the temple. And then, the temples were closed because of COVID-19. While I knew closing them was not personal, it felt deeply personal. It felt as though the Lord was leaving me to bear this burden alone. Holidays were the worst. I knew families were gathering and celebrating, but I wasn't. Depression and anxiety set in, and my feelings of isolation, loneliness, and abandonment intensified. Many nights my prayers were simply, "Father, help me. I can't do this."

One night as I lay crumpled to the ground, I saw an image of Christ hugging Mary and Martha on a book next to my bed, and I wanted that so desperately. I said "Father, I need a hug. I need to feel arms around me. I need to know that I am not alone."

It was this specific prayer that began the healing of my heart. I suddenly felt arms around me. I knew this experience was a blessing from heaven. I understood that Heavenly Father had not abandoned me; He was there and aware of me. After that experience, I began to recognize His hand all around me. As I did, I began to feel peace. My darkness became light and my healing began. I have learned that I have to choose, every day, to believe He will be there to bless and sustain me. I have to make a conscious effort not to fall back into loneliness but to stand tall and move forward. I know now that I am not alone and am constantly being blessed by my Father in Heaven.

Christ and His light are stronger than any darkness that threatens to overtake you.

Christ says in 3 Nephi 17:7, "Have ye any that are sick among you? Bring them hither. Have ye any that are lame, or blind, or halt, or maimed, or leprous, or that are withered, or that are deaf, or that are afflicted in any manner? Bring them hither and I will heal them."

When you look at this painting, I hope you can feel and see the Savior's love. I purposely drew Christ standing taller with His arms encircling those around Him to represent His love for us and His desire to be with us and to heal us. We will never be left to face our trials alone.

When you read these experiences in the Book of Mormon and Joseph Smith—History, what emotions do they bring up?

What do these accounts teach you personally about your Savior and His love for you?

Chapter Seven

Receiving Strength from Above

The first time I heard the scripture, "Pray always, that you may come off conqueror; yea, that you may conquer Satan" (D&C 10:5), I was sitting in my ninth-grade seminary class. The words jumped out at me and I felt a surge of energy run through my body. I wanted to conquer Satan, and I wanted to feel closer to God. I remember thinking to myself, "What does this scripture mean exactly? Do I just have to say a prayer, or is there a specific kind of prayer?" At that point in my life, I didn't fully understand what prayer was or how to use it, but I felt a desire inside to figure it out.

Fast forward a year to when I received my patriarchal blessing. I was sitting in the home of my patriarch. I was nervous, and I didn't know what to expect, but when he placed his hands on my head, I instantly felt calm and ready. I listened intently to what he was saying. I wanted to make sure I heard every word. As I was listening, he said the words "pray always," and my mind stopped. I went from focusing on all of the words to just those two words: "pray always." It brought me back to that moment in my ninth-grade seminary class. The same desire I felt then filled my heart up again. I wanted to learn how to pray and how to pray always so that I could conquer Satan and find the strength and direction I needed daily.

I knew the basics of prayer—thanking God and asking for blessings—but I felt like there was more to it. If I wanted to conquer Satan and find strength, my prayers needed to be more earnest, so I prayed and asked God to help me learn how I could pray and what it means to pray always. With inspiration from the Lord, I decided that I was going to start praying for my friends at school. I prayed that they would have a good day and that they would feel loved. I prayed for them when they had tests or a big event happening, or when I felt like they needed support. Praying for my friends helped me to love them more and see them differently. It helped to take my focus off my fears and put it toward a greater purpose. I started to feel happier inside, and I found strength to keep moving forward. Praying for my friends helped me to better conquer Satan and any discouragement he tried to throw at me.

When I was a new missionary, I felt a lack of confidence in my abilities. One really cold night while my companion and I were out knocking on doors, I remember praying for some kind of comfort. I was so tired of feeling inadequate. I was reminded of my experience with prayer in high school, so I started praying more earnestly for my companion, for our investigators, for our members, and for the people I saw walking past us on the street. I prayed that they would have peace and guidance. I prayed that they would feel love and hope. And just like before, it took my focus off of my fears and put it toward a greater purpose. Prayer helped me to love people more, but it also helped me understand and focus better on my purpose as a missionary. Prayer gave me strength to push past the fears I carried as a missionary and conquer Satan.

When I became a mother, I worried I wouldn't be able to do enough for my boys. I wanted so much for them. My prayers changed. They became more intense as I pleaded with the Lord, more times than I can count, to please help me with my sweet boys. I look back on my life as a mother and can see that my prayers have been heard, and I have received the hope, knowledge, and strength I need to conquer Satan and withstand his blows.

My son Cooper was diagnosed with bipolar disorder at a young age. It has been difficult for him. One evening, while Cooper and I were talking, he said to me, "I wish I never had to deal with bipolar disorder. It makes me feel like I'm a bad person. I feel like no one likes me. I don't want it anymore. Why did God give this to me?"

I held him close and tried my best to help him understand that he is a good person and that people do like him. I told him bipolar disorder isn't a punishment from God but an opportunity to grow and draw closer to Jesus and Heavenly Father.

A few days after that experience, I had a thought come to me to invite Cooper to receive a father's blessing. We talked about it and decided that we would fast and pray together before the blessing. Watching Cooper prepare for this blessing was humbling. He faithfully prayed and fasted for comfort and peace. His heart desperately wanted to feel calm. I felt that same desperation. I just wanted Cooper to know how important and loved he was regardless of the mental illness he was carrying. I wanted him to know that his Father in Heaven and his Savior were aware of him and his load.

When the day of the blessing came, Cooper was ready for it. He eagerly sat down, and Mike placed his hands on his head. I don't remember all of the words Mike spoke during that sweet blessing, but I do remember that Cooper was told that even though the bipolar disorder was not going to be removed from him, God was aware of him, and that through Christ, it could be made lighter and easier. I just sat back and watched Cooper. When he got up from that blessing, his smile was bright and he walked away a thousand pounds lighter. He had just had his first experience with the power of God to conquer the lies and doubts Satan wanted him to give in to. Since that experience, Cooper has continued to rely on prayer to help him find strength and comfort.

Prayer, whether it's on our knees, in our hearts, or in keeping our focus on God, changes our perspective. It shuts down Satan's efforts. It gives us clarity. President Thomas S. Monson said, "Prayer is the provider of spiritual strength; it is the passport to peace."[3] I have felt that spiritual strength and peace in my own life as I have tried to remember to pray always. There is power in prayer.

We can trust in the Lord's promise in Doctrine and Covenants 19:38: "Pray always, and I will pour out my Spirit upon you, and great shall be your blessing."

Questions

How has prayer changed you and your relationship with your Savior?

If you feel that your faith in prayer is weak, what can you do to help strengthen it?

Chapter Eight

Hold Up Your Light

Your light is needed. The adversary wants you to believe that you have nothing to offer. The world is always in our faces, telling us that we will never measure up, but this could not be further from the truth. God created you to shine, to share, to be a light to those around you. You bring hope, strength, and comfort into others' lives. It is through us that God's plan of happiness comes to life.

Think about it. God gave us mouths so we could smile and speak kind and uplifting words. He gave us arms and hands so we could hug each other and wipe away tears. He gave us ears so we could hear, listen, and understand one another. He gave us emotion so we could love and reach out to our brothers and sisters.

Have you ever smiled at someone in the grocery store or complimented a stranger? Have you ever gone out of your way to lift someone else, to lighten his or her load? Have you ever held someone who is hurting in your arms or sent an uplifting message to someone in need? Have you ever taken time to listen to a child, a friend, a spouse, a family member?

All of these are ways you are allowing light to shine through you, to give God's love and hope to those around you. These seemingly simple acts have deep meaning and purpose. They give you an opportunity to grow, to draw closer to the Savior and Heavenly Father, and to hold up your light for the world.

One of my favorite things to do is to mountain bike in cold wintery weather. I love bundling up and feeling the crisp air on my face and body as I bike. I love smelling the air and listening to the sounds around me. I love feeling the snow under my bike tires, fresh and clean. But my favorite part of mountain biking in the cold weather is when the sun comes up over the top of the mountains or out from behind the clouds and the heat from the sun hits me, instantly warming me up. When my hands and feet and lips are frozen, the sun suddenly gives me new energy and a determination to keep going forward. I always try to take a minute and soak up all of the heat I can.

That same energy can be felt when we share our light with those around us. We can give hope and new energy to those around us when we have the courage to share our light. The Lord says in Matthew 5:16, "Let your light so shine before men." I have often wondered why our Heavenly Father asked us to do this. It can be tempting to hide our light from the world because it feels safer and easier, but I have learned that when I live my life hiding my light, my personal growth stops, my happiness dims, my motivation weakens, and my purpose fades. Keeping our light from those around us can feel safer, but it is actually dimming our personal light.

A few months ago, a good friend of mine sent me a text message asking me my favorite color. "Purple," I texted back. I didn't think much of her text after she sent it. I just put my phone down and continued with my day. A few hours later, I got another text from her asking if I was home. I answered simply, "Yes."

A few minutes after that, I heard a knock at my door. When I opened it, there was my friend standing with a single purple rose in her hand. She held it out toward me and said, "You have been on my mind today." I immediately teared up.

She then explained to me that when I responded that my favorite color was purple, she was worried that she wouldn't be able to find a purple rose. But she went to the store anyway, hoping for the best. She said as she walked into the store and over to the floral section, she saw one single purple rose all by itself. It seemed incredible, but she quickly bought it because she knew that it was meant for me. My sweet friend went out of her way to search for, find, and bring me a rose in my favorite color all because I was on her mind that day. This experience might sound simple, but her effort to bring me that rose lifted my heart and brought light into my day—and continues to still.

The Lord gives us opportunities every day to share our light. Are we taking them?

I love this reminder from Sister Camilla Kimball, who said, "Never suppress a generous thought."[4] You never know the good that can come from it.

Our Heavenly Father is asking us to share our light for many reasons: to have opportunities to draw closer to Him and our Savior, to help us develop Christlike love for ourselves and those around us, to learn to overcome temptations and put off the natural man, to strengthen our testimonies and help us understand our purpose.

I love what Heavenly Father is teaching us in Moses 1:39: "For behold, this is my work and my glory—to bring to pass the immortality and eternal life of man." This is happening through us. We are our Heavenly Father's hands, and He trusts us. When we share the light within us, we are helping to sweep away doubts, loneliness, fears, and heartaches. We are helping others to know that they are known and loved by Heavenly Father and Christ. We are helping to carve a path to the Savior and His Atonement.

Don't be afraid to share your light. Your light leads to Christ's light.

Questions

What is your first response when you feel prompted to share your light?

What will you do to overcome doubt and let your light shine?

Chapter Nine

The Atonement

In 2018, I was getting ready for an upcoming art show. The theme of the show was The Life of Christ. I wanted to paint scenes of Christ's life to help those who attended the show feel a connection with Him. I had already painted *Faith to Be Healed* and *Through His Light* when this beautiful image of the Savior kneeling at a rock and looking up to heaven came into my mind.

I went into my studio, pulled out my watercolor paper, drew out this image, and started painting. The moment I put my brush to the paper was the moment the Spirit took over. I knew exactly what colors to use and where the light should fall on Christ. I knew I needed to keep this painting clean and simple. I felt directed to leave the top of the painting open.

As I was painting this central moment in God's plan, I felt so close to Jesus. The thought "Christ did this for me" came into my mind over and over. I was overwhelmed with gratitude for Him, for His courage and love for each of us. The Spirit was so strong as I painted, and I thought, "I will never lose this feeling." Immediately after I finished the painting, however, I was overcome with shame and embarrassment. The words "This is not a good painting, and no one will like it" came to my mind, and all of the fears and insecurities I had been fighting to conquer for so long were suddenly front and center.

I hate to admit it, but I listened to those fears, and I found a place where I could hide the painting. I felt defeated. I had desired to paint something that would represent this pivotal moment in all eternity, but fear took over. As the day of the art show grew closer, the image of Christ kneeling at that rock looking up to heaven kept coming into my mind, and I would go back and forth from "Yes, I'll put this painting in the show" to "No, I'll leave it out."

Finally, the week of the art show arrived. I had all of the other paintings framed and ready to go when I received a clear thought to include *The Atonement*. I knew that even though I was nervous, I needed to step above that fear and put the painting in a place where people could see it.

When the night of the show came, *The Atonement* was the first painting people walked up to and the first one they asked about. I was humbled. Watching people's reactions to this painting and hearing how it made them feel surprised me, and that feeling I had experienced in my studio while I was painting returned. I felt the Spirit close to me that night, reassuring me that this was a good thing and that people would draw closer to Christ because of it.

I have often thought about the experience I had while painting *The Atonement*. The contrast of light and dark reminds me of the experience Moses had in Moses 1. Moses saw God face to face and talked with Him. God taught Moses that he is a son of God—He calls him that three times! He shows him the world and everyone in it. I can only imagine the light and joy Moses felt during this incredible experience. We learn, though, that immediately after God departed from Moses, Satan appeared to him, trying to take that light and joy from him. We learn how fear came over Moses momentarily; however, the moment he turned to God, he received strength.

With Satan trying hard to separate us from Jesus Christ, His light, and His Atonement, it is important to keep our focus on the Savior so when the doubts come flooding in, we can have the strength to overcome them. This life is all about overcoming, but we are not overcoming alone. We have the Savior. He is our friend. He will be by our side while we learn and walk forward.

I love what the Lord says in Joshua 1:9: "Be strong and of a good courage; be not afraid, neither be thou dismayed: for the Lord thy God is with thee whithersoever thou goest."

We can have confidence in our Savior, Jesus Christ. He is inviting us to come to Him and receive the blessings of His Atonement. He has overcome the world. He has delivered us because He loves us. Consider this quote from Elder Jeffrey R. Holland:

In His willing submission to death He took upon Himself the sins of the world, paying an infinite price for every sorrow and sickness, every heartache and unhappiness from Adam to the end of the world. In doing so He conquered both the grave physically and hell spiritually and set the human family free.[5]

Christ's Atonement covers all things.

When I look at this painting, I see a beautiful and powerful moment between Father and Son where all of the pain of the world is felt and yet all of the love and forgiveness and grace is given. Christ died for us. He suffered so we could overcome. Turn to Him. Give your fears, doubts, heartaches, and mistakes to Him, and allow Him to give you peace.

Questions

How have you felt the healing power of the Atonement of Jesus Christ in your life?

What emotions do you feel when you think of the Savior's sacrifice?

Chapter Ten

Come unto Me

Looking back on my life and the experiences that have helped strengthen my connection with Jesus Christ solidifies my testimony that God and the Savior love us and are focused on us. I can see where Their hands have directed me throughout my life, and it helps me feel Their love.

I have thought a lot about why we experience the things we do and what those experiences can do for us. My conclusion is that every experience we have can lead us to Christ. When I was younger, I thought my experiences were a punishment because I felt unworthy of anything good. As I have gotten older, however, I've come to understand that God doesn't work like that. Our experiences aren't punishments but opportunities to improve who we are and turn to Christ, a time to sit with God our Father and draw strength from Him through the Savior. Experience provides an opportunity to sit still, to ponder, to be removed from the world, and to recenter ourselves, again allowing us to come to Christ.

This life is a time for us to grow, prepare, learn, and become more like our Savior, so it makes sense that God would allow us to have experiences that can bring us to the Savior.

In the summer of 2021, I had an experience that helped me know Christ and Heavenly Father better. I grew up swimming competitively off and on until my sophomore year in high school. I picked it back up in 2016, and in February 2021, I decided I was going to do a 10k open-water swim. I had only done an open-water swim a couple of times, so swimming six miles in open water felt a little daunting, but I wanted the experience. I knew I would have to train hard, overcome fears, and push myself, but I also knew I could accomplish the goal. I made a training plan, got the gear I needed, and started training. For the next five months, I focused on getting myself ready. There were days when I loved it and days when I hated it, but the goal was always the same.

The night before my big swim, I asked Mike for a priesthood blessing. I had worked so hard, and I didn't want my anxiety to overtake my focus. In the blessing, I was told that I needed to put my faith in God and myself, and that this experience would help me to know God better.

As I got in the water and started swimming the next morning, I thought about the words of the blessing. I wanted to pay close attention to the thoughts and feelings I might have while I swam, and I tried to keep the question "How will this experience help me know God better?" in my mind.

The first mile came and went, and I hadn't had any new insight into how this would help me know God better. Same with the second, third, fourth, and fifth miles. But as I came toward the last half of the sixth mile, when my body was tired and I was eager to get to the shore, I was suddenly filled with immense gratitude. I started thinking about how my husband Mike had been paddling alongside me the entire time, and how our friends Travis, Courtney, and Emily joined in the paddling a little while later. I thought about Mike's parents and our son Cooper cheering for me from the shore, and how every time I stopped for food or water they would shower me with encouragement and excitement. I noticed that the gratitude I was feeling was helping me through that last half mile. When I got to the shore, I was greeted with loud cheers and big hugs from my family and friends, and I felt immense gratitude all over again. I had set this goal for myself, and when I had accomplished it, I was surrounded by people who loved me and were excited with me. I can't help but think of the parallel between this experience and our eventual return to God's presence.

As I look back on my swim now and all of the details that went into it, I understand better that Heavenly Father cares about what we care about. He is interested in our lives, and even though He isn't with us physically, He sends His love and support to us, whether that is through our friends and family or our feelings. God wants us to know that He is there and that He loves us.

President Thomas S. Monson said, "God's love is there for you whether or not you feel you deserve love. It is simply always there."[6]

I love the comfort and truth we are given in these words from a prophet. We are loved, period. It doesn't matter what we have done or what we are currently doing; we are loved. Remembering this truth will help us to continue forward on our path to Christ.

I love learning about the Savior and the example He set. His life testifies of His love for us and who we are to Him. When the Savior says, "Come unto me" (Matthew 11:28), He is inviting us to step away from the noise of the world and bring our lives and loads to Him and find refuge. He knows that it is through Him, and only Him, that we will find the peace we need. Coming unto our Savior and trusting Him can be difficult because it means letting go of what we know and what we are comfortable with. It means allowing Christ to be a part of all the details of our lives. It means setting aside our doubts and our fears about who we are and opening up our hearts to Him.

Our Savior wants us to have the faith to let go, place our lives in His hands, and walk forward with Him. He knows as we do this, we will feel our trust in Him increase, we will see the growth and change that will happen within us, and we will start to know Him on a more personal level. Choosing to come unto Him will become second nature.

Christ does not pick and choose who can come unto Him. In 2 Nephi 26:25 we read, "Behold, doth he cry unto any, saying, Depart from me? Behold, I say unto you, Nay; but he saith: Come unto me all ye ends of the earth." He is reaching out to ALL of us. In verse 24 we learn, "He doeth not anything save it be for the benefit of the world; for he loveth the world, even that he layeth down his own life that he may draw all men unto him. Wherefore, he commandeth none that they shall not partake of his salvation." His hands are continually stretched out toward every one of us.

Christ knows us. He knows our struggles and heartaches. He knows the pains we carry and the desires we have to change. He knows and understands our doubts and fears, and He is inviting us to bring all of it to Him.

"Come unto me, all ye that labour and are heavy laden, and I will give you rest. Take my yoke upon you, and learn of me; for I am meek and lowly in heart: and ye shall find rest unto your souls" (Matthew 11:28–29).

There may be times when we believe that we are not worthy to come unto Jesus Christ and that God is displeased with us and our life, but please remember that those thoughts do not come from your Heavenly Father. I find strength in these words given by President Boyd K. Packer:

> There is no habit, no addiction, no rebellion, no transgression, no offense exempted from the promise of complete forgiveness. Restoring what you cannot restore, healing the wound you cannot heal, fixing that which you broke and you cannot fix is the very purpose of the Atonement of Christ.[7]

Similarly, Elder Jeffrey R. Holland stated:

> However late you think you are, however many chances you think you've missed, however many mistakes you think you have made or talents you think you don't have, or however far from home and family and God you feel you have traveled, I testify that you have not traveled beyond the reach of divine love. It is not possible

for you to sink lower than the infinite light of Christ's Atonement shines.[8]

Their words teach us that we are loved, wanted, needed, understood, and valued by our Heavenly Parents and Savior. Let us reach toward Them because They are ever reaching toward us.

This painting, *Come unto Me*, is my testimony of the Savior and His love for all of us. I know that when we exercise our faith, put our trust in Him, and bring our lives to Him, we will find rest, healing, guidance, hope, strength, and peace. We will gain a deeper understanding of Christ and His Atonement.

Painting this image of the Savior inviting us to come unto Him was something I wanted to take my time on. I wanted it to feel warm and inviting. I wanted viewers to know that Christ is aware of them personally and that His hand is stretched out toward them always. I wanted the mark on His hand to be visible as a reminder that He suffered all things for them. Above all, I wanted them to feel the love the Savior has for them individually. I love the way His hand is stretched out, welcoming us to Him. I love the tender way He is looking over us, letting us know that we are His focus. I love the soft colors that surround Him; I feel they testify of His gentleness. I hope when you look at this painting, it helps you feel closer to your Savior. I hope the Spirit testifies to you that He is aware of you personally and that He is inviting you to come unto Him and find rest.

I love the scripture Doctrine and Covenants 19:23, in which the Lord states, "Learn of me, and listen to my words; walk in the meekness of my Spirit, and you shall have peace in me." I've always interpreted it as Christ saying, "I know this life is going to have its challenges, and I know you are going to stumble along the way, but I am here with you. Come unto me, do as I do, and everything will be okay."

I know as you come unto Christ and give your life to Him you will find the strength you need to continue to walk forward. I know the answers you seek through prayer will come. I know the hope and healing you need will be extended toward you, and I know as you reach for Jesus Christ, you will feel His perfect love for you.

Questions

What habits or practices can you give up so that you can more freely come unto Christ, and how will you let go of those things?

What can you start doing to more closely come unto Christ?

1. Boyd K. Packer, "Self Reliance," *BYU Speeches*, March 1975.
2. Dieter F. Uchtdorf, "The Love of God," *Ensign*, November 2009.
3. Thomas S. Monson, "Be Your Best Self," *Ensign*, May 2009.
4. In Bonnie D. Parkin, "Personal Ministry: Sacred and Precious," Brigham Young University devotional, February 13, 2007.
5. Jeffrey R. Holland, "The Only True God and Jesus Christ Whom He Hath Sent," *Ensign*, November 2007.
6. Thomas S. Monson, "We Never Walk Alone," *Ensign*, November 2013.
7. Boyd K. Packer, "The Brilliant Morning of Forgiveness," *Ensign*, November 1995.
8. Jeffrey R. Holland, "The Laborers in the Vineyard," *Ensign*, May 2012.

About the Author

After a chance meeting with an inspired fellow artist, Kate Lee modified her initial artistic direction to focus on works of inspirational watercolor. With a minimalistic style that conveys powerful family and gospel messages, Kate speaks to us through her art when words are insufficient. Kate and her husband, Mike, live in Utah with their two boys and two dogs.